National
Museums
Scotland

National Museum of Scotland
Guide

First published in 2012 by
NMS Enterprises Limited – Publishing
a division of NMS Enterprises Limited
National Museums Scotland
Chambers Street
Edinburgh EH1 1JF

Publication format, text and images
© National Museums Scotland 2012
(unless otherwise credited, see opposite)

ISBN: 978 1 905267 59 0

Publication layout and design by
    NMS Enterprises Limited – Publishing.
Cover design by Mark Blackadder.
Cover images of the Grand Gallery: front cover © National
    Museums Scotland; back cover © Andrew Lee.
Printed and bound in the United Kingdom by Bell & Bain
    Ltd, Glasgow.

National Museums Scotland has a Picture Library which holds thousands of images of the collections. Images are available to license for editorial use. Please contact the Picture Library for more details on 0131 247 4026.

For a full listing of NMS Enterprises Limited – Publishing titles and related merchandise: **www.nms.ac.uk/books**

ACKNOWLEDGEMENTS

Page 22 Sir James Young Simpson, image John Moffat, Scottish National Portrait Gallery; 24 Frances Teresa Stuart, National Portrait Gallery, London; 26 John Muir, image Library of Congress; 27 Thomas Stevenson, image Trustees of D. Alan Stevenson; 32 sika deer, tiger, Burmese python, image © Rob McDougall; 37 Earth in Space gallery, image © Andrew Lee; 42–43 Tibetan Prayer Wheel, image © Rob McDougall; 44 *A Very Hot Day* by Samantha Hobson, courtesy of the artist, Andrew Baker Art Dealer and October Gallery; figures and camp dogs, Wally Pwerle, 2006–2007, Living Lands gallery, image © Rob McDougall; 46 Ainu tray © Kaizawa Tōru; Dr Neil Munro, image © courtesy of Fosco Maraini; 48 Battle Dress © Vanessa Paukeigope Jennings, Kiowa/Tohono O'odham, 2007; 49 © Paa Joe, model of Mercedes coffin; 51 Ravanna, Demon King mask © Nepal Chaundra Sutrahu, 2001; 52 *Gubuka*, stingray sculpture © Dennis Nona, 2009; *Valley of Lar* poppies © Maryam Salour, 2009–11; *58 Standing Heech*, Parviz Tanavoli, 2007, acquired with the support of Charles Pocock FRAS and Meem Gallery; Tanavoli with his work *Big Heech Lovers*, Vancouver, 2008, © Parvis Tanvoli/photo: John Gordon; 59 *Mountains with gold decoration* © Kondō Yuzō, 1972; Kondō Takahiro with works from his *Orkney* series, Tokyo, 2008, image © Yamazaki Kenichi; 60 Preston Singletary at Indian Market, Santa Fe, 2008, image © Hulleah J. Tsinhnahjinnie; *Trance* © Preston Singletary, Tlingit, 2006; *To the Manor Sporran* © The Singh Twins, www.singhtwins.co.uk, 2000; The Singh Twins, image © www.singhtwins.co.uk; 67 We are grateful to the Society of Antiquaries of Scotland for permission to reproduce the portrait of Alexander Henry Rhind; 72 Electric violin © Starfish Designs, 2011; 87 *Corryvrechan Tapestry* © Kate Whiteford, purchased with assistance from The Scottish Arts Council/National Lottery Fund; 89 Figures in Early People gallery © Trustees of the Paolozzi Foundation, Licensed by DACS 2012; 91 City of Edinburgh Council/National Museums Scotland; 94 Mary, Queen of Scots [detail], artist unknown, after Francois Clouet, Scottish National Portrait Gallery; 97 Prince Charles Edward Stewart [detail], by Antonio David, 1732, Scottish National Portrait Gallery; 102 Reproduced by kind permission of Diageo on loan to the National Museums of Scotland; 104 John Rae, artist Stephen Pearce, Scottish National Portrait Gallery

While every effort has been made to acknowledge correct copyright of images where applicable, any unintentional omissions or errors should be notified to the Publisher, who will arrange for corrections to appear in subsequent editions.

Contents

Introduction

Dr Gordon Rintoul
Director, National Museums Scotland

Welcome to the National Museum of Scotland. On 29 July 2011, after three years of partial closure, we reopened our doors and the crowds surged into the transformed galleries of the former Royal Museum in Chambers Street, Edinburgh.

An amazing 20,000 visitors came on the first day. They created an electric atmosphere of excitement and participation. They revelled in the new displays and enjoyed the gloriously renovated Victorian architecture. The transformation has not only opened up the 19th-century museum, but united it firmly with the adjacent 20th-century building which tells the story of Scotland. It is a major landmark in the history of the organization which stretches back to Victorian ideals of education, and beyond those to the belief in the cultivation of knowledge and reason that characterized the Scottish Enlightenment.

This guide introduces all the galleries and highlights some special objects and their stories.

Our collections are vast and cover natural sciences, world cultures, European decorative art, science and technology, and Scottish history and archaeology. The galleries are arranged to reflect these subjects. They also present objects from different disciplines together, to complement their narrative and to create interesting juxtapositions. This draws on our strength as the largest multi-disciplinary museum in Scotland.

We have an extensive programme of special exhibitions and events; you can find up-to-date information on our website, or at the Museum itself.

The National Museum of Scotland is a wonderful place to visit, with lots to see and to enjoy for all ages. We hope that you will be entertained by the fascinating stories revealed through the magnificent and significant objects in our collections, and that you will return again and again to appreciate them.

Opening day at the transformed National Museum of Scotland, 29 July 2011.

Grand Gallery

When you arrive in the **Grand Gallery** of the National Museum of Scotland, you are in one of Scotland's most beautiful spaces. Its glorious Victorian architecture, the atrium with its glass roof, soaring columns and sweeping balustrades, was at the very forefront of engineering when it was designed by the Royal Engineer Captain Francis Fowke (1823–1865) in 1861. Fowke was also responsible for the great architectural designs of the Victoria and Albert Museum and the Natural History Museum in London. The **Grand Gallery** is a space full of light and air, with dramatic displays of objects in the **Window on the World** installation providing a foretaste of the galleries to come.

The space exemplifies the National Museum of Scotland, a place where the cultures of Scotland and the world meet, and the arts and sciences intermingle. It is the heart of the building from which great vistas open up to give you a sense of the scale and the scope of the displays. These are arranged by broad theme: the Natural World, World Cultures, Art and Design, Science and Technology and the History of Scotland.

You can appreciate immediately the visual impact of the large free-standing objects in the **Grand Gallery**, but each one also has a particular significance and story. In addition, they act as signposts, leading and enticing the visitor to discover the breadth, depth and richness of the collections.

Statue of James Watt

James Watt (1736–1819), from Greenock near Glasgow, was a pioneer of the Industrial Revolution; an inventor and mechanical engineer who changed the face of manufacturing. This marble statue shows Watt drawing one of his most significant inventions, the double-acting beam engine. These efficient steam-powered engines were used to drive machinery in workshops and factories across the world.

As a young man, Watt set up a business making mathematical instruments. He then began to experiment with steam power, improving on previous designs.

This statue was commissioned from the leading monumental sculptor of the day, Francis Chantrey. Showing Watt deep in thought, it was praised for its insight into 'the inner workings of a powerful mind'.

James Watt, by Sir Francis Chantrey (1782–1841), marble, 1827–1832
Lent by Heriot-Watt University Museum and Archive

Printing press, D. & J. Grieg, Edinburgh, c.1860

Columbia printing press

The Columbia printing press (opposite) was designed by an American, George E. Clymer, in 1813 to print newspapers. Clymer's press was not a great success in the United States of America, so he brought his design to Britain where it proved more popular.

This press was made in Edinburgh by D. & J. Grieg around 1860, when Edinburgh was a major centre of the publishing industry. It was purchased by the Museum in 1865 and used to print labels for nearly 100 years, until 1964.

Inchkeith Lighthouse lens

David A. Stevenson designed this dioptic lens in 1889 to update the lighthouse on the island of Inchkeith in the Firth of Forth. The lighthouse itself had been built in 1803 by Robert Stevenson and his father-in-law, Thomas Smith, to protect shipping coming into the Port of Leith.

For five generations the Stevenson family designed and built lighthouses around the coast of Scotland. They also exported their ideas successfully across the world. Their designs saved lives and cargo from being lost in dangerous passages on rough and rocky coastlines.

This lens was in use at Inchkeith Lighthouse until 1985, when the last lighthouse keeper was withdrawn and the light automated.

Lighthouse lens, Chance Brothers, Birmingham, and James Dove & Co., Edinburgh, 1889

Drinking fountain

This cast iron drinking fountain was made in the 1880s by the Glasgow firm, Walter Macfarlane and Co. The fountain has a fretwork dome and is covered with designs drawn from nature, including storks, swans and flowers. Decorative ironwork such as this was very fashionable in the 19th century, as changes in manufacturing techniques made it possible to produce cast iron that was strong and could be shaped into complex designs.

Walter Macfarlane and Co. was Scotland's most important manufacturer of ornamental ironwork. The company was well-known for making public drinking fountains, bandstands and other architectural ironwork. Macfarlane exported products around the world and some examples of their ironwork still survive in places as diverse as a bank in India, a theatre in Brazil, and Raffles Hotel in Singapore.

Drinking fountain and pavilion,
Walter Macfarlane and Co., Glasgow, 1880s

Temple statue, sandstone, Ancient Nubia,
100–50 BC

Statue of Arensnuphis

This statue (opposite) stood guard at the entrance to an ancient Nubian temple dedicated to Isis, goddess of fertility, motherhood and magic. His clothing and headdress identify him as the god Arensnuphis.

Ancient Nubia (now modern Sudan) was situated along the River Nile, to the south of Egypt, and close links were established between Nubia and Egypt as early as 4500 BC. The Egyptians were particularly interested in Nubia's rich supply of ebony, ivory and gold.

The two civilizations shared cultural traditions: they both worshipped the same gods and preserved the bodies of their dead kings in pyramids. Nubian pharaohs ruled Egypt between 780 and 656 BC.

Between 1909 and 1914, Professor John Garstang of the University of Liverpool excavated the Nubian city of Meroe. He found the stones of this statue scattered among the remains of a temple. This Museum helped to pay for Garstang's expedition and so acquired a share of his finds.

Feast bowl

This feast bowl comes from Atiu, one of the Cook Islands in the South Pacific. In 1871, Parua, the high chief of Atiu, presented the bowl to a female chief in the Society Islands. Men from Atiu sailed 500 miles by canoe to deliver it.

The bowl was inherited by Titaua, a Tahitian princess. In the 19th century, Tahiti attracted its share of Scottish businessmen seeking their fortunes in the Pacific. Titaua's hand was sought first by the Scot John Brander, with whom she managed a huge plantation and labour business. After his death she married George Darsie, who came from Anstruther.

In 1892, Titaua and Darsie retired to his home

town in Scotland. Darsie sold this bowl to the Museum in 1895, after Titaua's death. She was buried in Anstruther Easter churchyard.

Holding up to 300 gallons, the bowl originally would have been used at large communal feasts to serve *poi* – a dish made from sweet potato, yams, taro or plantain, mashed up and mixed with coconut milk. Feasts were important in traditional Cook Islands' culture; having plenty of food was a sign of prosperity.

Cook Islanders were expert wood-carvers, and this boat-shaped bowl was carved from a single piece of tamanu wood, also known as island mahogany.

Feast bowl, *umete,*
Cook Islands, before 1870s

Buddha Amida

Devotees of the Buddha Amida chant his name to pray for rebirth in the western paradise, the Pure Land. The faith developed in Japan in the 12th century and continues to be one of the largest Buddhist groups there today.

This bronze statue shows Amida seated on a lotus pedestal in an attitude of meditation known as *dhyana mudra*, with the hands resting in the lap, palms facing upward, and the tips of the thumbs touching the index fingers. He wears a monastic robe and his hair is drawn up to form the 'hump of perfect wisdom'. On the halo behind him are the 25 guardians chosen to protect all true believers.

James Douglas Fletcher (1857–1927), a Scottish entrepreneur, acquired this sculpture in 1902 for his home, Rosehaugh, on the Black Isle, Scotland. He owned tea, coffee and rubber plantations in Ceylon (now Sri Lanka) and spent a considerable amount of money refurbishing Rosehaugh with treasures from overseas.

Ritchie clock

James Ritchie set up a clockmaking business in Edinburgh in 1809. This clock, a half-scale model of the clock commissioned for St Giles Cathedral, Edinburgh, was made for the Museum in 1921 by James Ritchie's grandson. He described the clock as the finest he had ever crafted.

The clock has a striking mechanism using tubular bells which sound the Westminster chimes. The gravity escapement, which keeps the train of clockwork moving regularly, was invented by Lord Grimthorpe, who devised it originally for the clock in Big Ben, London.

Clock, James Ritchie and Sons, Edinburgh, 1921

Buddha, Japan, 1800–1850

Giant deer

This is the first complete skeleton of a giant deer to be discovered. It was found on the Isle of Man in 1819 and brought to Edinburgh by the Duke of Atholl.

Giant deer survived until 7700 years ago in western Siberia. They grew up to 2 metres tall at the shoulder, with antlers spanning up to 3.5 metres wide. This specimen was smaller, probably because it lived on an island with limited food supplies.

In 1821 the skeleton was given to the University of Edinburgh, which had one of the world's leading natural history collections. These collections were transferred in 1865 to the Edinburgh Museum of Science and Art, one of the predecessors of National Museums Scotland.

The keeper of the collections, Professor Robert Jameson, sent a sketch of the skeleton to French zoologist Georges Cuvier, who published it in 1823 in his famous book *Ossemens Fossiles*. Through his study of fossils, Cuvier was the first to demonstrate extinction as a natural process. Discoveries like this skeleton confirmed his theories.

Giant deer skeleton, *Megaloceros giganteus*,
Isle of Man, 12,300 years old

Window
on the world

Window
on the world

Window on the World

The **Window on the World** installation runs the height of the **Grand Gallery** and is a breathtaking construction of over 800 objects, sourced from the natural world, the decorative arts, science and technology, world cultures and archaeology. The display celebrates the range and scope of the Museum and its capacity to draw from, and juxtapose, objects from many disciplines and cultures.

Chesterfield wine-cooler

This superb piece of Georgian silver was crafted in London by two leading goldsmiths of the day, Paul de Lamerie and Paul Crespin.

It was made for Philip Dormer Stanhope, 4th Earl of Chesterfield, as part of a silver service supplied by the Royal Jewel House for his role as Ambassador to The Hague in 1728. The wine-cooler is decorated with representations of the seasons and engraved with the royal arms and cypher of King George II. One of a pair, the other is in the Victoria and Albert Museum.

Mackintosh lamp

The Scottish architect and artist Charles Rennie Mackintosh designed this lamp as part of a commission to redecorate the home of a Glasgow shipping magnate in 1902. Its simple but strong form in unusual materials, and its innovative shape, reflected the Art Nouveau style. It was created from copper with leaded glass panels and was part of Mackintosh's scheme of interior design for the whole house.

Wine-cooler, Paul de Lamerie and Paul Crespin, London, 1728 (Level 5)

Supported by The Art Fund, National Heritage Memorial Fund, and others

Lamp, Charles Rennie Mackintosh (1868–1928), Glasgow, 1902 (Level 1)

Blue John vase

This vase is thought to be the world's largest artefact carved from Blue John. Known as *bleu et jaune* in French, the banded blue and yellow fluorite became known as 'Blue John' in English.

Mined in the Derbyshire Peak District, the mineral was highly fashionable in the 1760s. This vase was carved by James Shore in the late 1840s, its form derived from ancient Greek pottery.

During the early 19th century, carvers at Matlock in Derbyshire competed with each other to produce the largest vases, but the best veins of Derbyshire fluorite were exhausted shortly after this vase was made.

Vase, Blue John fluorite, made by James Shore (*c.*1815–*c.*1849), England, 1840s (Level 5)

Blaschka models

During the late 19th century, master glass artist Leopold Blaschka, and later his son Rudolf, produced beautifully detailed glass models of plants and sea creatures for natural history museums around the world.

Blaschka trained as a jeweller and goldsmith in the Czech Republic before moving to Dresden in Germany in 1863. His models replicated the form, colour and translucency lost when marine creatures were preserved in ethanol. At a time when aquariums were rare and underwater photography impossible, these models were the closest that most people came to experiencing such animals.

Glass models by Leopold Blaschka, 1860s (Level 3)

Whale art

In 1843 Robert Jameson, Professor of Natural History at the University of Edinburgh, asked the captain of the whaling ship *Woodlark* to bring back the jaw-bones of a sperm whale for study. On the long voyage home from the Far East, the sailors engraved large images, known as scrimshaw, into each jaw-bone of their captured whale, showing the hunt in extraordinary detail. At 5 metres long, these are thought to be the largest examples of scrimshaw in existence. The Professor, however, was less than impressed and turned the scrimshaw to the wall.

The University's natural history collections, including the jaw-bones, were transferred to the Museum in 1865 as one of its founding collections.

Wylam Dilly, locomotive model

This working model of the *Wylam Dilly* locomotive, at 1:3 scale, was made in 1885. It is one of the earliest surviving models to be constructed in the Museum workshops.

The actual *Wylam Dilly*, designed and constructed by William Hedley in 1813, is displayed in the **Connect** gallery (page 81). One of the world's two oldest surviving steam locomotives, it was named after the Wylam Colliery where it was used to pull coal trucks along the Wylam Wagonway to the river, near Newcastle upon Tyne.

The whale hunt, scrimshaw image on whale jaw-bone, 1843 (Level 3)

Wylam Dilly, working model, 1885 (Level 3)

The Pembridge Helm

This 14th-century head-piece belonged to one of King Edward II's knights, Sir Richard Pembridge, who fought in the Hundred Years' War between England and France. It is of the type which would have been worn at the Battles of Crecy in 1346 and Poitiers in 1356.

For most of the century, the helm's excellent protective qualities made it the best in military technology. However, its weight and minimal field of vision led to it being eventually superseded. Only three such helms, including this one, survive.

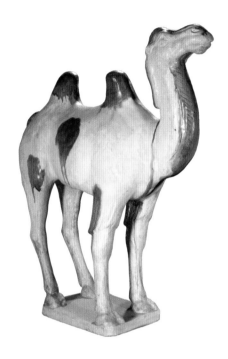

Chinese tomb figure

This earthenware figure of a Bactrian camel was part of the ritual of burial in ancient China and dates from the Tang Dynasty, 618–906. Chinese tombs contained objects needed for the afterlife, such as vessels, weapons, furniture, ornaments, jewellery and ritual objects. The tomb of the Emperor Qin Shi Huangdi (reigned 221–210 BC) at Xi'an, for example, was surrounded by a life-sized terracotta army. During the following centuries, the earthenware figures enclosed in tombs included horses, camels, servants, soldiers, musicians and even model buildings.

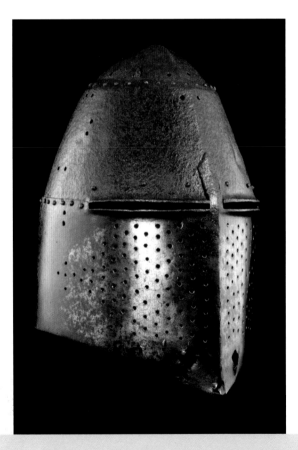

Tomb figure of a Bactrian camel, Tang Dynasty, China, 8th century (Level 3)

The Pembridge Helm, England, pre-1375 (Level 5)

The Millennium Clock

This clock tower is an extraordinary construction, originally created for the Scottish Millennium Festival. Over 10 metres high and made out of wood, metal and glass, it commemorates the human story of the millennium, and the chaos of the last century in particular.

The clock tower was created by four artists – Eduard Bersudsky, Tim Stead, Annica Sandström and Jürgen Tübbecke – who took their inspiration from Bersudsky's previous work in kinetic sculpture. It comes to life on the hour, as its many figures whirl into action with music and light effects.

Mechanical clock tower, made by Eduard Bersudsky, Tim Stead, Annica Sandström and Jürgen Tübbecke, Glasgow, 1999

Discoveries

Situated off the **Grand Gallery** is **Discoveries**. Here you can see a wide selection of objects that demonstrate the nature and range of Scottish achievement by innovators, inventors, diplomats, military leaders, adventurers, scientists and academics. The displays recognize the enormous impact of Scots abroad and their contribution to the British Empire.

Well-known names such as John Muir, pioneer of conservation, and Alexander Fleming, discoverer of penicillin, are included alongside less familiar figures such as Alexander Dalrymple, inventor of the Admiralty chart, and Charles Stuart, Duke of Richmond and Lennox, courtier to King Charles II.

Some of the objects in this gallery were generously given by their original owners to extend the national collection; others descended through generations and many hands before being acquired by the Museum. This gallery offers a distillation of their stories.

Tibetan armour

Tibetan lamellar armour was used from the 14th to the 20th centuries. It consisted of small plates of iron, the lamellae, joined together with leather thongs. This suit is one of the finest known examples. It was sold to the Museum in 1908 by a soldier, Colonel Frederick Bailey (1882–1967), who had fought in Tibet.

Tibetan lamellar armour, as used from the 14th to 20th centuries

21

An Assyrian king

One of the most important objects in the collection, this panel once decorated the walls of a palace of the Assyrian king, Ashurnasirpal II (c.883– 859 BC). Its limestone relief shows the king as a bearded high priest facing a court official.

Ashurnasirpal II was a very successful military campaigner, and some of his victories are listed in the cuneiform script. Such panels are an important, and often the only, source of information about the ancient Assyrian empire.

In the 19th century the panel came into the ownership of Sir James Young Simpson, the Scottish obstetrician who pioneered the use of chloroform to relieve pain during childbirth. Simpson had a keen personal interest in ancient history and was a member of the Society of Antiquaries of Scotland. He built up his own collection and gave this panel to the Society in 1865. The Society's collections laid the foundations of today's National Museums Scotland.

King Ashurnasirpal II (above right) and court official, limestone panel, Assyria, 9th century BC

Sir James Young Simpson (1811–1870), c.1861

An Egyptian priest

The coffin base and mummy in this gallery are highlights of the Museum's rich collection of Egyptology. They are thought to belong to a distinguished senior priest at Karnak, Iufenamun, who lived during the early 22nd Dynasty (mid- to late 10th century BC).

The coffin base, which is elaborately decorated in the Theban style, has been united with a lid of similar style and period, belonging to a woman who may have been a relative. Her full name was Tjentweretheqau, but she was also known as Tamut.

The Scottish engineer Colonel Sir Colin Scott-Moncrieff played a significant role in the enormous engineering projects to dam the Nile in the 1880s. After his return home with these artefacts, he eventually gave them to his old school, Edinburgh Academy. Recognizing their importance, the school passed them to the national collection in 1907.

Coffin lid, Egypt, early 21st Dynasty
(late 11th or early 10th century BC)

Coffin base, Egypt, early 22nd Dynasty
(mid- to late 10th century BC)

Colonel Sir Colin Scott-Moncrieff (1836–1916)

The Duke and Duchess of Richmond and Lennox

King Charles II re-established the grandeur of the monarchy, and his Restoration court conducted its affairs in sumptuous style. This spectacular man's suit, made of silk and silver tissue, was worn by Charles Stuart, Duke of Richmond and Lennox, as a Knight of the Garter. The ancient Order had been reinstituted by the King and, as a favoured courtier, the Duke was one of the first to be knighted in 1661.

The Duke's marriage in 1667 to the beautiful Frances Teresa Stuart caused the King great consternation as he had wanted her for himself. Nonetheless, the elaborately-crafted French toilet service on show in the gallery, made in the style of Louis XIV and lavishly equipped to meet feminine beauty needs, is thought to have been a gift from Charles II in the 1670s, demonstrating her continued welcome presence at court.

Both the suit and toilet service remained in the hands of Scottish descendants of the Duchess for generations until acquired by the Museum.

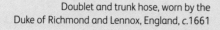

Doublet and trunk hose, worn by the
Duke of Richmond and Lennox, England, c.1661

Frances Teresa Stuart, portrait (detail) by William Wissing
and Jan Van der Vaart, oil on canvas, 1687
Lent by the National Portrait Gallery, London

Alexander Dalrymple, sea chart designer

In 1795, Alexander Dalrymple was made the first Hydrographer to the Admiralty.

An experienced seaman, Dalrymple deplored the absence of proper standardized charts of the oceans. As Hydrographer he created a reliable format to record and publish the necessary data, and he is credited with the creation and design of the Admiralty charts, which were developed further over the next 150 years to map the world's seas.

Dalrymple's work ensured that the Royal Navy had the most accurate charts available and helped pave the way for the rapid growth of the British Empire.

The portrait shows Dalrymple in the uniform of an East India Company sea officer, aged about 28, in his home at Newhailes outside Edinburgh. Apart from a pencil sketch taken in old age, it is the only likeness in existence of this influential Scotsman.

Alexander Dalrymple (1737–1808), portrait by John Thomas Seton (c.1735–c.1806), oil on canvas, c.1765

Supported by The Art Fund and National Museums Scotland Charitable Trust

25

John Muir, National Parks pioneer

This fossil wood, *Araucarioxylon arizonicum*, is 210 million years old and comes from the Petrified Forest National Park, Arizona.

Scottish-born naturalist John Muir emigrated to America with his family in 1849. As an adult he developed his passion and knowledge of nature and was instrumental in campaigning for the preservation of the American wilderness.

Muir recognized the importance of the Petrified Forest in Arizona, which contains America's largest and most spectacular deposits of petrified wood. The fallen trees of the ancient forest were buried in silt and volcanic sand under water. Over time, water-borne silica slowly replaced the wood, creating the colourful and startling shapes of the petrified logs.

Muir championed the creation of national parks to safeguard areas such as the Petrified Forest. He supported the United States National Park Bill which set up Yosemite and the Sequoia National Parks in 1890.

Fossil wood, *Araucarioxylon arizonicum*, from Petrified Forest National Park, Arizona, USA, 210 million years old, donated by John Muir

John Muir (1838–1914)

The Lighthouse Stevensons

This optic, designed by Thomas Stevenson, was exhibited in the Paris exhibition of 1867. It demonstrated his design for condensing light which would be used for the Tay Leading Light, one of two lights used to guide shipping into the River Tay on the east coast of Scotland.

For five generations the Stevenson family were extraordinarily successful as lighthouse engineers. Between 1786 and 1938 they designed and built, or rebuilt, every lighthouse around the coast of Scotland.

Such success drew worldwide attention and their business took them around the globe. In 1868 they exported an entire lighthouse system to Japan.

The Stevensons continually introduced new ideas, developing more powerful lenses and stronger structures, to enable lighthouses to be built in the most remote and dangerous places.

Lighthouse optic, Chance Brothers and Company, Birmingham, 1866

Thomas Stevenson (1818–1887)

Natural World

The Wolfson Galleries of the Natural World

Through the arch at the eastern end of the **Grand Gallery** you can see the head of a *Tyrannosaurus rex* apparently peering through.

This giant dinosaur leads you into a stunning series of galleries about the Natural World which cover animal life and the evolution of our planet. These galleries ask the big questions about how the world works and what we know about it.

In the **Animal World** galleries you will find a giraffe stretching its neck to reach a leafy morsel, a great white shark swimming towards you, baring its razor-sharp teeth, and two gaudy peacocks battling with their sharp thorn-like spurs for the chance to mate. Hundreds of fascinating animals from around the world have been brought together to illustrate the extraordinary variety of animal life on Earth.

We share our planet Earth with many millions of species of living things, from minuscule viruses and bacteria to mighty whales and trees. The **Animal World** galleries examine how animals have evolved over hundreds of millions of years, and are continuing to evolve and adapt to ever-changing climates and habitats on, above and within the Earth.

The story of the evolution of the incredible diversity of animal life on Earth is told in three galleries, **Animal World**, **Animal Senses** and **Survival**, linked by a spectacular array of swimming and flying animals in the **Wildlife Panorama**.

Next to **Animal World**, two galleries tell the story of our planet. **Earth in Space** explores Earth's place in the universe and how our understanding of it has developed, while **Restless Earth** investigates the geological processes that constantly shape and reshape the planet.

Animal World

In the centre of the gallery, dramatic groupings of animals on open display introduce the main themes of behaviour and interaction with the environment. The groupings also introduce the theme of evolution and how species have changed and adapted over time.

Extremes of habitat are demonstrated by the polar bear of the Arctic and the Bactrian camel of the desert. The sheer scale of the largest mammals is shown by the enormous African elephant that stands in the middle of the jaw-bones of a blue whale, the biggest animal ever known.

Hunting and feeding methods are illustrated by the startlingly large skeleton of the giant ground sloth which survived until about 10,000 years ago, weighed up to 5 tonnes and was 5.5 metres long. Only the giraffe, stretching his neck to reach foliage, stands taller.

African elephant, *Loxodonta africana*, and jaw-bones of a blue whale, *Balaenoptera musculus*

Giraffe, *Giraffa camelopardalis*

Opposite page: The **Natural World** galleries.

A lion and lioness, with two cubs, stand in their family group (above). A tiger leaps towards a Sika deer, while an enormous Burmese python slithers along the ground, demonstrating different ways of moving (below).

Themes of habitat, food, movement, defence, protection and reproduction are explored further in the displays and interactives, inviting you to test your knowledge and compare your abilities with those of animals.

Lion family, *Panthera leo*

Sika deer, *Cervus nippon*
Tiger, *Panthera tigris*
Burmese Python, *Python molurus bivittus*

Overhead, a procession of animals can be seen swimming
and flying in the **Wildlife Panorama**, dramatically suspended
from the height of the gallery. Sounds and images from the
wild are projected on large screens, adding excitement and
colour to the displays.

Animal Senses

This gallery shows how animals sense their environment and communicate with each other.

All animals have their own ways of sensing, some similar to us, but many very different. Some have sharper sight, keener smell, super-sensitive touch or, in some cases, senses that are completely beyond the human experience. They might use ultrasound or electricity to navigate or to detect prey, while others need to hide themselves with camouflage, or create a showy display to attract a mate.

This page:
The male Indian peacock, *Pavo cristatus*, spreads its upper tail to attract a mate.

Opposite page
(clockwise from below left):
Just before homing in on a wood mouse or vole, the barn owl, *Tyto alba*, closes its eyes to avoid injury from the surrounding twigs and plant stems.

Each feather-shaped antenna of the male wild silk moth, *Antheraea polyphemus*, has 55,000 pheromone receptors.

The duck-billed platypus, *Ornithorhynchus anatinus*, was the first mammal discovered to have an electric sense.

Hammerhead sharks, *Sphyrna mokarran*, have a highly-sensitive electric sense.

Leaf insects, *Phyllium giganteum*, have evolved a remarkable similarity to leaves.

The lesser Egyptian jerboa, *Jaculus* sp., like other jerboas, has very sensitive middle ears that amplify the sounds of potential predators.

Survival

Change has taken place over millions of years as species have adapted to survive or else died out completely. This gallery explains how evolution works. It includes displays of fossils millions of years old, and threatened and extinct species.

The ability of a species to adapt to its environment is key to its survival. Evolution and extinction are constantly happening, changing the diversity of life on Earth.

Mass extinctions have wiped most animal life from the Earth at least five times, creating many natural gaps for survivors that have evolved and diversified to fill them. The best known occurred 65 million years ago with the end of the dinosaurs, after which mammals diversified and spread into every habitat on Earth.

Today the impact of human activities on the planet is accelerating and threatens the survival of life as we know it. A 'roll call' of extinction, showing currently endangered species, is listed alongside evidence of the threat to animal life from pollution, habitat loss, hunting and persecution, alien predators and disease.

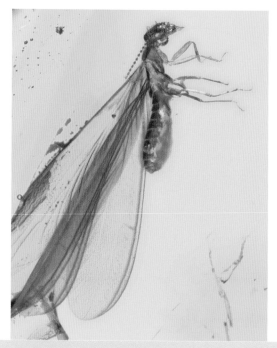

Dodo, *Raphus cucullatus* – extinct
Dodos, from the Indian Ocean island of Mauritius, were last seen in 1662.

Steller's sea cow, *Hydrodamalis gigas*, skull – extinct
Naturalist Georg Steller noted the existence of the sea cow in 1741. By 1768 it had been hunted to extinction.

Fossil termite in Mexican amber, 25 million years old

Earth in Space

An early 20th-century orrery, a magnificent glass globe representing the planets in our solar system and the constellations of the night sky, greets you at the entrance to this gallery.

Here you will find examples of the technology that helped mankind to investigate the big questions of the universe.

The **Earth in Space** gallery.

Above: Orrery, Sendtner, Munich, 1913

Scientists analyse evidence from Earth and Space in their attempts to understand the universe and the origins of life. You can see examples of the instruments and charts with which they have tried to measure and record Space and time through the ages.

The earliest is an astrolabe, dating from the 11th century, which was used to find time and direction from the stars. It was crafted in Spain and is the oldest surviving signed and dated astrolabe made in Europe.

In contrast is the red bulk of the SCUBA camera of the 1990s. The SCUBA (Sub-millimetre Common User Bolometer Array) was built at the Royal Observatory, Edinburgh. It was one of the most important modern astronomical tools. When it came into use in 1996, nothing else could see galaxies so far away. It saw over 10 billion light years distant, three-quarters of the age of the universe.

Astrolabe, by Muhammad ben as-Saffâr, Cordova, Spain, 1026–1027

Submillimetre Common User Bolometer Array (SCUBA), Edinburgh, 1996

Rocks and minerals illustrate the story of the formation of matter and remind you of the importance of Scottish geology.

A large sample of the oldest rock on Earth, the 4-billion-year-old Acasta gneiss from Canada, is on show beside an example of Lewisian gneiss, at about 3 billion years old the oldest rock in Scotland. Other rocks contain embedded fossils which provide clues about the origins and development of life on Earth.

Many beautiful minerals are also on display, and a film, *Universal Odyssey*, takes you on a journey through time and space.

Liversidge nugget

In 1888 the distinguished scientist Archibald Liversidge called this nugget of crystallized gold, found in Australia, the finest in existence. Its shape resembles the outline of Great Britain.

Leadhillite, Scotland

Caledonite, Leadhills, Scotland

Brewsterite, Strontian, Scotland

Acasta gneiss, Northwest Territories, Canada

Gold nugget, Ballarat, Victoria, Australia

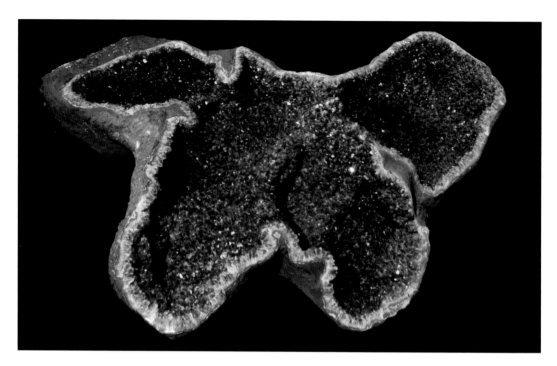

Restless Earth

This gallery examines the dramatic processes which continually mould and shape the Earth's surface. Its centrepiece is a pair of enormous amethyst geodes formed in cavities of lava 130 million years ago.

The displays show how the Earth has constantly changed over the millennia and how continents and oceans have come and gone in response to the continual movement of tectonic plates across the Earth's surface.

Amethyst geode

During volcanic activity, trapped gas bubbles in lava can merge to form large cavities. Over time, mineralized solutions seep into these voids and crystals, such as amethyst, are deposited. Crystal-lined cavities are called geodes.

Amethyst geode, Rio Grande do Sul, Brazil, 130 million years old

Reptile fossil, *Mesosaurus tumidum*, Goias State, Brazil, Permian, 290–248 million years old

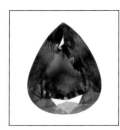

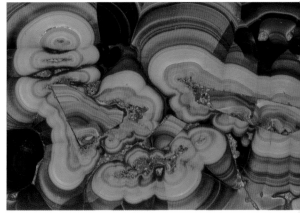

Since its inception the Earth has been steadily cooling. This, combined with time and gravity, has caused our planet to develop distinct layers and different kinds of rock, some of which have the beautiful patterns and colouring illustrated here.

Volcanic eruptions, earthquakes and erosion all have different impacts, leaving in their wake clues to the forces that have shaped and changed our world. Natural processes create exceedingly beautiful minerals, some of which are then further refined to become the glittering gem stones on display.

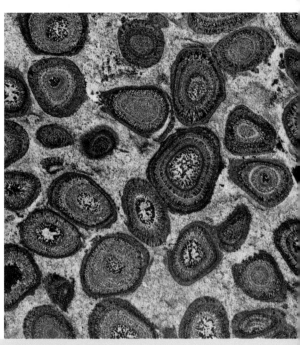

Sulphur, Sicily, Italy

Tsavorite garnet, Tsavo, Kenya

Fire opal, San Juan Del Rio, Central Mexico

Above right: Contact of granite and gneiss, detail, Aberdeenshire, Scotland

Middle: Malachite, detail, Siberia, Russia

Above: Orbicular granodiorite, detail, Australia
This polished specimen contains distorted spherical structures called orbicules. The centre of each orbicule represents a growth point around which crystals grow in a radical and concentric structure. The orbicules then settle under gravity to form this spectacular rock.

World Cultures

The Adèle Stuart Galleries of World Cultures

Since it was founded in the mid-19th century, this Museum has always aimed to show the world beyond Scotland. In these galleries devoted to World Cultures, you can see objects from an extraordinary range of countries. They are grouped by theme rather than geography or historical narrative. This gives you an insight into the different cultures and provides some thought-provoking juxtapositions. It emphasizes the diversity of cultures, their creativity, their interaction and their state of flux. You can also listen to stories, watch films and try some games and interactives.

Many of the objects came to the Museum as a result of the experience of Scots abroad. Explorers, missionaries, traders and settlers all contributed to the collections. The first director, George Wilson, set out with deliberate intent to build an international network, from his appointment in 1855 until his early death in 1859. Wilson and subsequent directors made great use of contacts with businesses such as the Hudson's Bay Trading Company in Canada.

For years many of these items lay in store. They have been rediscovered, reinterpreted and, most importantly, extended to cover the contemporary, and are a key feature in the transformed National Museum of Scotland.

You reach the galleries through the southern arches off the **Grand Gallery**. They extend over three levels, from **Living Lands** and **Patterns of Life**, up to **Performance and Lives** and **Facing the Sea**, and finally **Inspired by Nature**, **Artistic Legacies** and **Looking East**.

Prayer wheel house, made at Kagyu Samye Ling Monastery, Scotland, Europe's oldest and largest centre for Tibetan Buddhism, Rokpa Developments, Eskdale-muir, Scotland, 2009; prayer wheels, Nepal, 2009

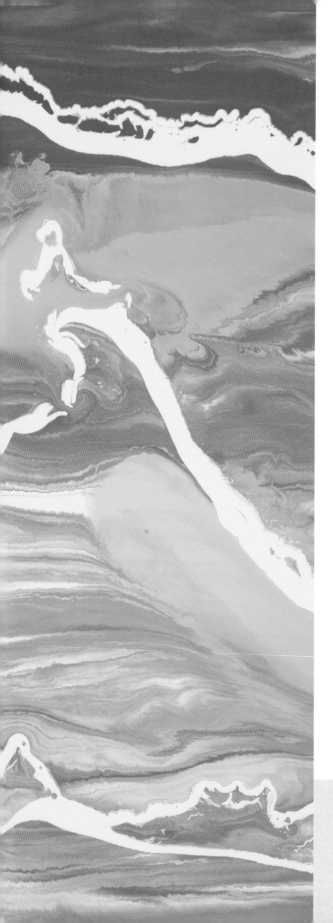

Living Lands

A Tibetan prayer wheel, a monumental carved memorial pole from the northern Pacific coast, a storyteller's face mask from the Arctic, and a contemporary painting from Australia inspired by the heat of the desert, are some of the highlights you will encounter in **Living Lands**.

The gallery reflects how landscape and climate influence people's lives and how they respond to and interact with them. It shows life in the high mountain plains of Tibet, on the lush coast of the Pacific, in the cold wastes of the Arctic, and in the heat of the Australian desert.

Figures and camp dogs, Wally Pwerle, Northern Territory, Australia, 2006–2007

A Very Hot Day, Samantha Hobson, acrylic on canvas, Australia, 2008

Gwich'in man's summer outfit

A sumptuous outfit with many beads and dentalium shell was a sign of a man's wealth and a woman's skill in the Northwest Territories in 19th-century Canada.

Tibetan nomad

Nomadic women living in the eastern regions of the Tibetan Plateau regularly wore spectacular outfits with heavy ornaments until the 1940s. Today such outfits are worn at festivals.

Thunderbird Transformation mask and outfit

The dance performances of the Nuu-cha-nulth and Kwakwaka'wakw people of western Canada are inherited privileges which dramatically re-enact events from oral histories. The Thunderbird mask opens to show a human face, referring to the transformation of an ancestor to help the Great Chief during a terrible flood. Its creator, Calvin Hunt, danced the mask and outfit in Port Hardy, Vancouver Island, before they were sent to Scotland in 1999.

Costume decorated with shell ornaments, Amdo, Tibet, late 19th to early 20th century

Man's summer outfit, Gwich'in, Northwest Territories, Canada, c.1862

Thunderbird Transformation mask and outfit, Calvin Hunt (born 1956), Kwagu'l/Mowochaht, British Columbia, Canada, 1999

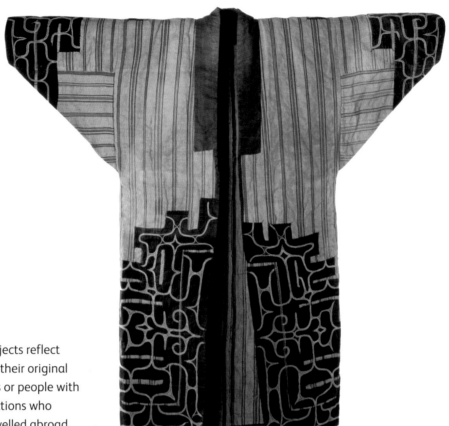

Many of the objects reflect the interests of their original collectors: Scots or people with Scottish connections who worked and travelled abroad.

Ainu robe and tray

A Scottish doctor, Neil Gordon Munro, spent nearly 50 years living in Japan and became interested in the Ainu people of the northern coast and islands. They were an ancient indigenous group whose customs were threatened by change. Munro amassed evidence of their culture, dress, hunting equipment, craft and religion, and gave it to the Museum (above and left).

Ainu robe, Hokkaido, Japan, 19th to early 20th century

Ainu tray by Kaizawa Tōru Nibutani, Hokkaido, Japan, 19th century

Dr Neil Munro (1863–1942)

Yup'ik mask

Isobel Wylie Hutchinson (1889–1982), from Edinburgh, became an inveterate Arctic traveller. She is thought to be the first British woman granted permission to enter Greenland in 1927. Among other items collected by her, the Arctic displays include this extraordinary mask from Nunivak Island off Alaska, of the kind used in the ceremonial telling of stories by the Yup'ik people during the long dark winter.

Whale hunt hat

The great explorer, Captain James Cook (1728–1779), was the first British sea captain to sail around the world in a lone ship. On his last voyage he sailed across the northern Pacific and, in 1778, was the first European to land on Vancouver Island, the traditional territory of the Nuu-chah-nulth people. Cook collected this native hat (left), decorated with scenes showing the local whale hunt.

Mask, Yup'ik, Nunivak Island, Alaska, USA, 1930s

Hat with images of the whale hunt, Vancouver Island, Canada, late 18th century

Chief Maguinna wearing a whale hunt hat, from a drawing of 1791 by Thomas de Suriā.

Patterns of Life

The overarching themes of this gallery are the cycle of life from birth to death and the identities and values conveyed through particular clothes and possessions.

Objects from the Americas, Africa, the Middle East and Asia are broadly grouped by continent. You can see a Native American outfit of the early 19th century, associated with Chief Wana'ata, the elaborately layered dress worn by a Zoroastrian bride in Iran, the modest style but rich fabric of a court dress from Bhopal, India, and colourful robes from Nigeria, Africa.

Animal skin painted shirt and leggings, associated with Lakota Chief Wana'ata, possibly Gros Ventre or Assiniboine people, USA or Canada, early 19th century

Battle Dress by Vanessa Paukeigope Jennings, Kiowa/Tohono O'odham, Oklahoma, USA, 2007

Woman's full court dress, including cap and shawl, Bhopal, India, mid-19th century

There are many objects of special significance for ceremonial or religious reasons, including the beautiful altarpiece (right) to the farming god of the Igbo people, Nigeria, and the flamboyant Mercedes Benz coffin as used by the Ga people of Ghana in the late 20th century.

Model of Mercedes-Benz coffin, Accra, Ghana, late 20th century

Altarpiece showing a Chief and his two wives, clay, Igbo people, Nigeria, c.19th century

Performance and Lives

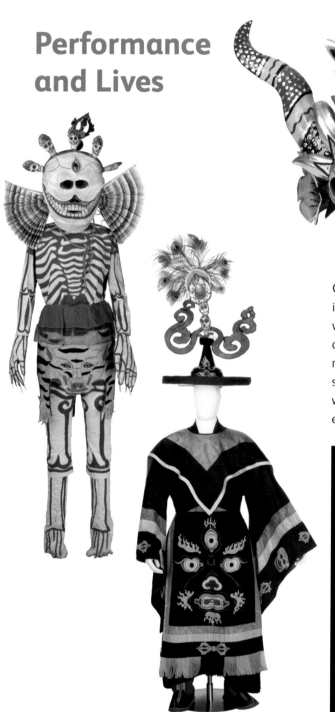

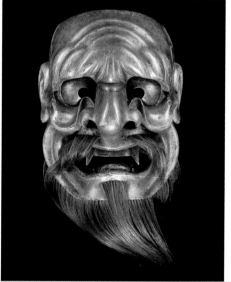

Ceremony and performance are important aspects of our lives. All over the world, people watch and participate with a sense of occasion and wonder in events ranging from community festivals to sacred rituals. Sound and colour combine with music and costume to heighten the experience.

Buddhist Cham Dance, skeleton and Black Hat costumes, as worn by Tibetan Buddhist monks, Tibet, 19th to early 20th century

Devil dance mask, Bolivia, mid-20th century

Nō mask, carved by Deme Mitsunao, painted by Deme Mitsutaka, Japan, 1690–1715

This gallery shows examples of ceremony and performance from around the world. These include the flamboyant costumes of the traditional Buddhist Cham Dance intended to bring blessings on the community; and a dramatic series of masks ranging from the frivolity of the Venetian carnival, to the solemnity of Japanese Nō drama, and the colourful multi-faced Indian Demon King, Ravanna.

Jean Jenkins

This gallery also includes over 100 musical instruments, many of which were collected by Jean Jenkins. American-born Jenkins was an unusually adventurous and determined museum curator. Her ability to persuade people to perform and to provide her with examples of their instruments enabled her to create a remarkable archive of musical traditions in Africa, the Middle East and Asia. You can hear a selection of her recordings in the gallery.

Ravanna, Demon King mask,
made by Nepal Chaundra Sutrahu, Edinburgh, 2001

Venice carnival mask, Zago E. Molin' design, Italy, c.2005

Jean Jenkins (1922–1990)

Facing the Sea

The Pacific is the largest expanse of water on the planet, scattered with thousands of islands where people belong as much to the sea as the land. This gallery explores the diversity and history of these ocean people.

The stories told here encompass the lives and customs of these maritime people and the changes wrought upon the region after its exploration and settlement by Europeans.

The collections range from Lapita pottery from Fiji, dated to *c.*900 BC, to modern sculpture by a Torres Strait islander, Dennis Nona. There is also a remarkable cloak created from the red and yellow feathers of the tiny honey creeper bird, made for Hawaiian royalty in the 19th century, and a protective suit of coconut fibre from the Kiribati Islands.

Gubuka, stingray sculpture, by Dennis Nona, Torres Strait Islands, 2009

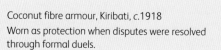

Coconut fibre armour, Kiribati, *c.*1918
Worn as protection when disputes were resolved through formal duels.

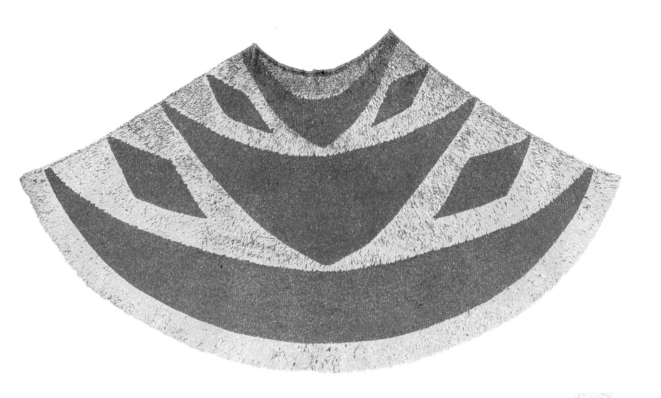

Canoes

Two canoes are suspended dramatically in the atrium space. The Maori, or *waka*, canoe has a modern stern post carved in perspex. You can hear the story of how Maori artist, George Nuku, created this sternpost in an imaginative treatment fusing modern and ancient craftsmanship.

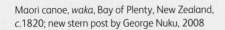

Maori canoe, *waka*, Bay of Plenty, New Zealand, c.1820; new stern post by George Nuku, 2008

Cloak made from feathers of honey creeper bird, Hawaiian Islands, early 19th century

53

Cook's clock

This astronomical regulator clock, made by John Shelton, was part of the equipment of Captain James Cook on his first voyages of exploration in 1769. It was used to observe the Transit of Venus, the passage of the planet across the sun. Measuring its duration helped to establish distances in the solar system.

Robert Louis Stevenson

The Scottish writer Robert Louis Stevenson sought the warmth of Samoa for the good of his health. After his death there, his mother brought treasured possessions back to Edinburgh, including mats and fans (see above).

God of the sea, Cook Islands, early 20th century

Astronomical regulator clock, by John Shelton, England, 1756

Fan, Samoa, late 19th century, associated with Robert Louis Stevenson (1850–1894) (left)

Inspired by Nature

The relationship between artist and nature takes different forms. Some artists may be inspired to depict nature, others to use its materials, some to create entire imaginary worlds. For many, their work represents an association of nature with the divine.

This gallery explores the relationship between man and nature as it is expressed in art, demonstrating how, for more than 2000 years, nature has been a source of artistic inspiration.

Drawing on ancient, historical and contemporary works from around the world, the gallery is presented in four sections: **Art and nature**, **Nature used and reflected**, **Imagined worlds** and **Seeing the divine**.

Saint George slaying the dragon, embroidery, detail, by Phoebe Anna Traquair (1852–1936), 1907

Haniwa horse tomb figure, Osato district, Japan, 7th century

55

There are some astonishing pieces in this gallery. These include a headdress made almost entirely of kingfisher feathers for Chinese theatre, a selection of netsuke, the small intricately carved toggles used as fastenings in Japan, and some beautiful examples of modern work such as the *Valley of Lar* ceramic poppies by Iranian artist Maryam Salour.

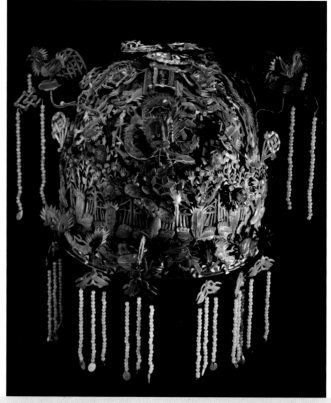

Oni, a demon, drinking sake, netsuke, signed Hojitsu, Japan, 19th century

Raijin, Thunder God, netsuke, signed Nagotsugu, Japan, 19th century

Valley of Lar poppies, glazed earthenware, by Maryam Salour (born 1954), Tehran, Iran, 2009–2011

Theatrical headdress made from blue kingfisher feathers, China, Qing Dynasty, 19th century

Ancient Greek pottery often depicts traditional tales of man's heroism and supremacy against the monsters of nature. The continuity of such tales throughout history is emphasized with objects such as the embroidery of *Saint George slaying the dragon* (page 55), made by leading Arts and Crafts artist, Phoebe Anna Traquair in the early 20th century.

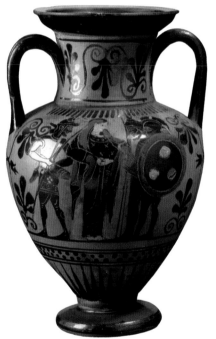

Nature as a creative and destructive force is often associated with religion and particular deities. This can result in striking and forceful works of art representing the power of the gods and their stories, such as those of the Hindu gods and goddesses Shiva, Parvati and Ganga included in the gallery.

Kalighat painting, India, late 19th to early 20th century
The goddess Ganga descends to earth. The goddess personifies the holy river, the Ganga (Ganges).

The Ninth Labour, Heracles fights the Amazons, amphora, Greece, 6th century BC
Ancient myth depicted on a storage vessel.

Artistic Legacies

Artists take their inspiration from many sources and this gallery examines artistic traditions from different cultures and their relationship to the work of contemporary artists. The voices of these artists commenting on their work shed further light on its cultural context.

It is a telling demonstration of the capacity of art and artists to evolve, to borrow from other times and places, and to adapt materials and techniques to new purpose. By engaging with them, we can widen our understanding of other ways of thinking and celebrate the diversity of their achievement.

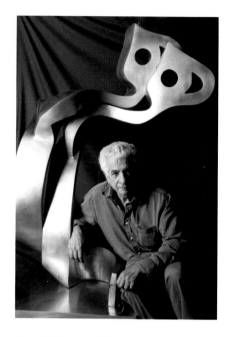

Parviz Tanavoli

A modern Iranian sculpture, *Standing Heech* by Parviz Tanavoli, stands next to traditional Iranian tiles. Tanavoli's works draw on the rich heritage of Iran, transforming two-dimensional scripture into three-dimensional sculpture.

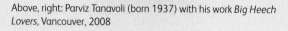

Above, right: Parviz Tanavoli (born 1937) with his work *Big Heech Lovers*, Vancouver, 2008

Standing Heech, by Parviz Tanavoli, Iran, 2007
Supported by Charles Pocock and Meem Gallery

Frieze tile with moulded Arabic inscription, Persia, 13th century

Twentieth-century pieces by the Japanese Kondō family, distinguished potters for three generations, can be found close to traditional blue and white porcelain.

Kondō family

The Kondō family are three generations of potters from Kyoto. Working within the *sometsuke* tradition of cobalt blue and white porcelain ceramics, each has developed an individual style.

In the case of Kondō Takahiro (below), the range of his work has been extended into sculpture and metalwork, as well as pottery.

Kondō Takahiro (born 1958) stands beside examples of his work.

Mountains with gold decoration, plate by Kondō Yuzō (1902–1985), Kyoto, Japan, 1972

Traditional blue and white porcelain plate with birds, Japan, 1800–1850

Preston Singletary

Singletary transfers to glass the iconography, forms and symbolism central to the Northwest Coast carving tradition. *Trance* (below) is based on the traditional rattle used by shamans in south Alaskan Tlingit communities. The bird is an oyster-catcher, and the figure on its back is part-animal, part-human, in the midst of painful transformation.

Modern artists also include Native American Preston Singletary (Tlingit) working in glass, and the Singh Twins, whose paintings are created in Britain but influenced by the Indian miniature tradition.

The Singh Twins

The portrait above, by the Singh Twins, is from a series on Lord Singh of Butley (Sirdar Iqbal Singh).

Preston Singletary at Indian Market, Santa Fe, 2008

Trance, Preston Singletary (born 1963), Tlingit, USA, 2006

To the Manor Sporran, miniature painting, The Singh Twins, 2000

The Singh Twins

The range of time and place allows for some fascinating juxtapositions. Works from ancient cultures such as Greece, Benin and the Nasca of Peru stand close to modern pieces from Africa and North America.

Benin bronze

In the ancient African Kingdom of Benin, the royal arts glorified kingship. The sacred person of the Oba or King was traditionally commemorated in sophisticated bronze sculpture.

Double-spout bottle with spotted cat figure, Nasca, Peru, AD 200–300
The ancient Nasca civilization flourished along the river valleys of the arid south coast of Peru from the 1st to the 7th centuries AD.

Left, below: Amphora of black-figure pottery showing a mythic scene of battle, by the 'Antimenes Painter', Greece, 520 BC

Above: Commemorative head of an Oba, Benin, Nigeria, 19th century

Looking East

The Lady Ivy Wu Gallery

The three East Asian civilizations displayed in this gallery – China, Korea and Japan – developed highly distinctive artistic, technological and cultural traditions. In this gallery you can see the evidence for this through the ancient, beautiful and modern objects on display. You can also see how, as trade developed between East and West, Chinese and Japanese craftsmen began to produce objects for the Western market.

Kabuki actor as Edo wardsman, by Utagawa Kunisada, colour woodblock print, Japan, 1862

Porcelain bowl made in celebration of the Empress Dowager Cixi's 60th birthday, from Jingdezhen kilns, Jiangxi Province, China, Qing Dynasty, 1894

China

China's rich legacy of art and culture is one of the world's great cultural heritages. The focus of the displays here is on China's last dynasty, the Qing (1644–1911). You can glimpse something of the splendour of the Qing imperial court through objects such as thrones, imperial robes, jades and porcelains.

Objects illustrating aspects of life in China feature in displays exploring the world of the scholar, eating and drinking, burial, and the European export trade.

Recent Chinese history is addressed through objects from the era of the Cultural Revolution (1966–1976) which illustrate the extraordinary ideologically-based visual culture of that period.

Longpao (dragon robe), man's court dress, China, Qing Dynasty, late 19th century

Japan

The spectacular armour of a samurai warrior (right) dominates the Japanese display.

The military élite of the samurai class effectively ruled Japan from 1185 until 1868. Samurai means 'one who serves' and a strict code of conduct was followed, 'the way of the warrior'. The armour on show dates from the relatively peaceful period of the early 19th century and was more for show than fighting.

Other displays showcase different aspects of life in this period and include a large number of fine netsuke, the intricately-carved toggles used as fastenings for clothing and boxes. There is also a changing selection of wood-blocks from the Museum's extensive collection.

The continuity of the Japanese tradition of crafts-manship is demonstrated by some intriguing modern objects, ceramics, glass and jewellery from the lively world of studio crafts.

Bronze group, cockerel on a tree-stump and a hen with three chicks, made by Ōtake Norikuni, Japan, c.1893
This is typical of pieces made for the great international exhibitions of the Victorian era.

Suit of Samurai armour, Japan, early 19th century

Korea

Korean civilization is celebrated for its unique tradition of ceramic production, a tradition dating back millennia.

Ceramics on display include the major elements of this proud cultural tradition, with examples from the Three Kingdoms Period (300–668), the Goryeo (918–1392) and Joseon (1392–1910) Dynasties. There are beautiful examples of the distinctive Korean ceramics techniques: the famous green glaze and underglaze inlay technique of the Goryeo and the soft underglaze blue of Joseon.

Stoneware lotus-shaped cup and stand, Korea, Goryeo Dynasty (918–1392)

Supported by The Art Fund

Rice bowl, Korea, Joseon Dynasty (1392–1910), 17th century

Porcelain storage jar, Korea, Joseon Dynasty (1392–1910), 15th century

Supported by The Art Fund

Ancient Egypt

The Ancient Egyptian empire survived for nearly 3000 years, making it one of the longest ever known. For most of that time it was a highly conformist society. This is reflected in the artefacts that survive; their style barely changes throughout the whole period.

Ancient Egyptians believed in the afterlife. They thought that the soul would continue to need the body after death. This led to the creation of elaborate tombs to provide sanctuary for these bodies, carefully preserved through mummification and housed in beautifully-painted coffins, surrounded by grave goods and wall paintings.

The displays, with their remarkable range of material, coffins, mummies, jewellery, pottery, furniture, amulets, texts, paintings and grave goods, give you some understanding of the sophistication of this ancient civilization.

Coffin of Khnumhotep, son of Nebtu, Deir Rifeh, Middle Egypt, second half of 12th Dynasty (c.1800 BC)
This is the earliest coffin in the Museum's display.

Alexander Rhind

Serious European interest in Ancient Egypt developed in the 19th century. The Scot Alexander Rhind, regarded as a pioneer in field archaeology, insisted on the precise recording of excavations and documentation of finds.

Rhind spent three winters in Luxor and donated the bulk of his superb collection of finds to the Society of Antiquaries of Scotland, one of the predecessors of today's National Museums Scotland. Rhind also contributed a unique late Roman Period double coffin for two young boys, Petamun and Penhorpabik, which he purchased for the collection.

Coffin base of Petamun and Penhorpabik, Thebes, late Roman Period, c.AD 174–200

Alexander Henry Rhind (1833–1863)

William Flinders Petrie

One of the collection's great treasures came through the Museum's association with the pioneering archaeologist Professor (later Sir) William Flinders Petrie (1853–1942) who led a series of excavations in the early 1900s. In 1909 his team uncovered the remains of a young woman and child with an extraordinary wealth of gold jewellery and grave goods at Qurna, Thebes. This appeared to be the royal burial of a Queen and her child, and is now thought to be the only intact royal burial group from Ancient Egypt on display anywhere outside Egypt itself.

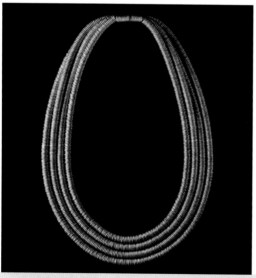

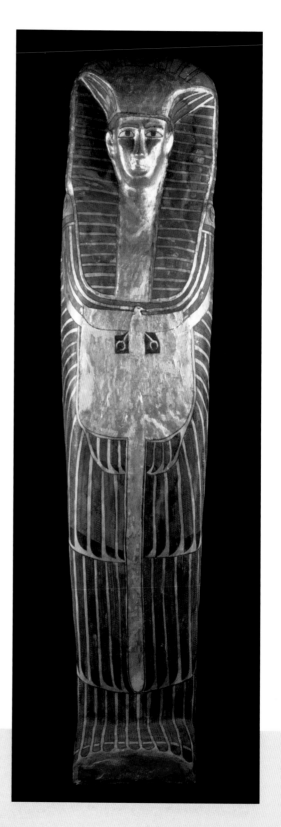

The 'Qurna Queen'
Woman's gold jewellery (above) and coffin (right) of a woman, Qurna, Western Thebes, 17th Dynasty
(c.16th century BC)

68

Art and Design

In these galleries – **Art and Industry**, **European Styles** and **Traditions in Sculpture** – you will find different aspects of the decorative arts: the relationships between design and art and industry, the development of different European styles, and the contrasting traditions of Western and Eastern sculpture.

From its opening in 1866 until 1904, when it became the Royal Museum, the Museum was known as the Edinburgh Museum of Science and Art and collected accordingly. The second director, Thomas Archer, took a keen personal interest in the decorative arts and, often in conjunction with the Victoria and Albert Museum in London, set out to build an ambitious collection between 1864 and 1885. He and subsequent directors took particular advantage of the opportunities offered for acquisition from the enormous international exhibitions of the Victorian era, as well as soliciting many gifts and loans.

The result today is an extended collection of European decorative art which represents excellence and creativity in metalwork, ceramics, glass, furniture, woodwork, dress and textiles. In these galleries, you can appreciate the scope and range of the collection, from the medieval era to the present day.

Summer, gesso and wood panel, detail, Margaret Macdonald Mackintosh (1864–1933), Glasgow, Scotland, 1904

Art and Industry

As new technologies, materials and methods of manufacture have developed and combined with traditional skills, they have contributed to the appearance and operation of everyday objects. As industrialization increased during the Victorian age, this cross-fertilization accelerated. In this gallery you can see how it influenced the production of luxury and mass-market items from the mid-19th century to the present day.

Dish in the Persian style, signed Leon Parvillé Studio, France, c.1873

Loving cup and cover, designed by Edward Spencer (1873–1938), Artificers' Guild, London, England, 1911
The Artificers' Guild was one of a few commercially successful craft guilds.

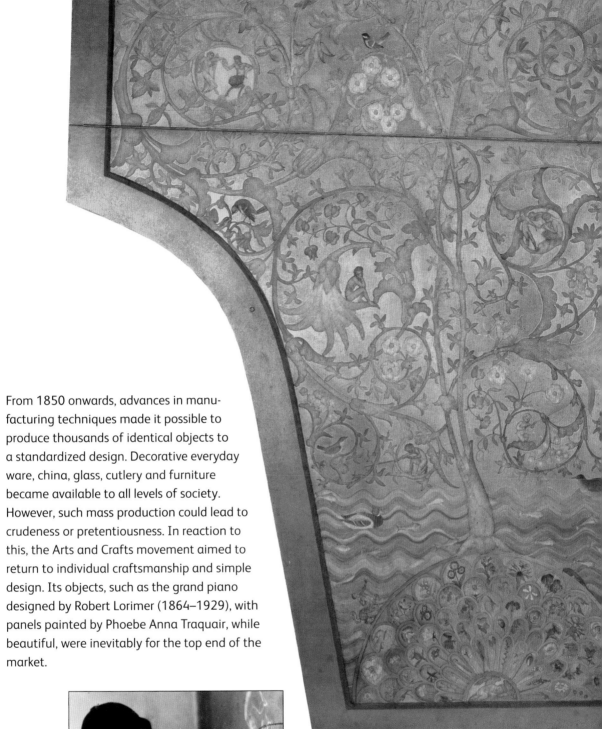

From 1850 onwards, advances in manufacturing techniques made it possible to produce thousands of identical objects to a standardized design. Decorative everyday ware, china, glass, cutlery and furniture became available to all levels of society. However, such mass production could lead to crudeness or pretentiousness. In reaction to this, the Arts and Crafts movement aimed to return to individual craftsmanship and simple design. Its objects, such as the grand piano designed by Robert Lorimer (1864–1929), with panels painted by Phoebe Anna Traquair, while beautiful, were inevitably for the top end of the market.

Lid of grand piano, painted by Phoebe Anna Traquair, for Frank Tennant, Lympne Castle, Kent, England, 1909–1911

Phoebe Traquair (1852–1936)

Industrial advances in communication and technology have had an enormous impact. They have driven the design and creation of entirely new objects such as telephones, radio, television, cars, planes and perhaps the most revolutionary object of the 20th century – the computer.

Steve Jobs (1955–2011) and his friend Steve Wozniak built their first commercial computer in Jobs' parents' garage in 1976. Although the monitor and keyboard were sold separately, the Apple 1 was the first fully pre-assembled computer. A rare survivor from the 200 that were made is on display.

Apple 1 personal computer, computer board (in case), monitor and keyboard, USA, 1976

Electric violin, made by Starfish Designs (Scotland) Ltd, 2011

European Styles

This gallery traces the major changes and influences in European style over the last 700 years. It includes spectacular items of silverware, furniture, dress, textiles, porcelain, sculpture and glass.

Maiolica dishes (above and left), made for the Calini family of Brescia, by Nicola da Urbino, Italy, c.1525

Da Urbino was the greatest of the story painters working with the newly-popular maiolica earthenware during the Renaissance.

Created in the 18th century, this white porcelain lion is the largest piece of Meissen ever made. Because the clay was modelled too thickly, cracks opened up on its body and legs during firing. These and other objects show artists experimenting with different materials and methods.

Trade and cultures from outside Europe influenced artistic developments. Furniture in the chinoiserie style of the late 17th century demonstrates the contemporary fascination with the East. A fine rococo vase (above), decorated with a charming and complicated design of birds, flowers and animals, made by the Chelsea Porcelain Factory, shows how the art of the manufacture of fine porcelain was absorbed from China.

Porcelain lion, Meissen, Germany, c.1732–1735

Reliquary casket, Limoges, France, early 13th century
This outstanding example of the technique of enamel developed at Limoges portrays the journey of the Three Kings to worship the Christ Child.

Perfume vase, Chelsea Porcelain Factory, London, c.1756

Patronage and commission have always been important to artists. Collectors have indulged their personal tastes for many reasons: to enhance their homes and reflect their status, as an act of conscious encouragement, or purely for private pleasure.

In the mid-19th century, Hamilton Palace, now demolished, housed Scotland's largest art collection in private hands. Alexander, 10th Duke of Hamilton (1767–1852), was a great collector and also an admirer of Napoleon. He was once the owner of this elaborate travelling service (above). It was made for the sister of Napoleon, Princess Pauline Borghese, by the leading silversmith of the day, Martin-Guillaume Biennais.

Ewer, Saint-Porchaire, France, c.1545–1560

An example of the elaborate style of Saint-Porchaire ceramics, once owned by the collector Horace Walpole, 1717–1797.

Nécessaire de voyage, travelling service with items for dining, toilette and sewing, made for Princess Pauline Borghese by Martin-Guillaume Biennais (1764–1843), Paris, France, c.1803

Supported by The Art Fund and The National Heritage Memorial Fund

Emperor Napoleon's tea service

Alexander, 10th Duke of Hamilton, also collected a magnificent silver-gilt tea service made in 1810 by the silversmith Martin-Guillaume Biennais for the Emperor Napoleon and his second wife, the Archduchess Marie-Louise of Austria. Today, some elements of the service are in the National Museum of Scotland and some in the Louvre, Paris.

Arthur Balfour's overmantel

The large ornate overmantel, *The Garden of the Hesperides*, was completed in 1900 by leading Arts and Crafts enameller, Alexander Fisher, for the Scottish home of Arthur Balfour, shortly before Balfour became Prime Minister. This commissioned piece attracted much attention and praise.

One of a pair of double salts from a tea service made for Emperor Napoleon, silver-gilt, in part designed by Charles Percier, supplied by Martin-Guillaume Biennais, Paris, France, 1810

The Garden of the Hesperides, overmantel, Alexander Fisher (1864–1936), London, England, c.1899–1900

Supported by The Art Fund, Wolfson Foundation and National Museums Scotland Charitable Trust

Traditions in Sculpture

An array of figurative sculpture fills one of the top balconies of the Grand Gallery.

From earliest times, sculptors have created works intended to inspire devotion, to tell stories, to commemorate individuals, or to capture beauty in a lasting form. These reflect the different traditions of their cultures.

This gallery contrasts Classical and Christian sculpture with those of the Hindu and Buddhist traditions.

For the former, it includes examples from the ancient world, the Renaissance and religion, as well as figures portrayed from life.

For the latter, it shows the diversity in the pantheon of gods and goddesses of Hindu belief in contrast to the focus on the monumental figure of the Buddha in that tradition.

Hercules and Iole, bronze group by Ferdinando Tacca (1619–1686), Florence, Italy, *c.*1650–1660

Buddha, hornblende schist rock figure, Gandhara School, India, AD 200–300

Science and Technology

This group of galleries – **Connect**, **Communicate** and **Shaping our World** – gives you the opportunity to look at, and try out, different kinds of science and technology. In **Connect** you can even take a Formula 1 racing car for a simulated drive around Scotland!

This sense of participation and engagement is very much in line with the intentions of the Museum's founding director. The origins of today's National Museums Scotland lie in part in the Industrial Museum of Scotland, founded in 1854. Its first director was George Wilson, Professor of Technology at the University of Edinburgh, who was appointed in 1855. In his report of 1857 he outlined his vision, stating that, 'An industrial museum cannot be complete without illustrations of the existing state of the useful arts [i.e. technology] among the nations of the world'.

Although Wilson died before the Industrial Museum opened in 1862, he created a strand of enduring importance in its approach to collecting. Today the collections cover developments in science, technology, communications and transport. This suite of galleries offers you the chance to see something of their scope, ranging from the enormous Boulton and Watt engine, one of the oldest surviving beam engines in the world, to the prizes awarded to the great Scottish scientist Sir James Black (1924–2010) for his development of beta-blocker drugs.

Connect

The enormous mass of the Boulton and Watt steam engine dominates the gallery. It represents the great advance in the economic generation of power from steam made by the Scottish-born engineer James Watt and his partner Matthew Boulton in the late 18th century.

The steam engine is complemented by the black bulk of the *Wylam Dilly*, one of the world's two oldest surviving steam locomotives, and the tall spire of the Black Knight rocket, a relic of British competition in the arms race of the 20th century.

All the exhibits are supported by information stations where you can explore what makes the objects work and the stories behind their development. You can also take part in a number of quizzes to see where you stand on some of today's issues of diminishing natural resources, cloning and human impact on the environment.

Steam engine, by Boulton and Watt, 1786
This steam engine was built from a design by James Watt, and produced by Watt and his business partner Matthew Boulton. It was used to pump water and grind barley at a brewery in London until 1884.

Dolly the Sheep

The first mammal to be cloned artificially, in a breakthrough by a Scottish research institute, now looks out quizzically from her rotating plinth.

Dolly was born on 5th July 1996 at the Roslin Institute and survived for 6 years. Her biological mother was a 6-year-old Finn Dorset ewe and her surrogate mother a Scottish Blackface ewe.

Wylam Dilly

Named after Wylam Colliery where it was used, this steam locomotive, built in 1813, was used instead of horses to haul coal trucks along the Wylam Wagonway to the river, near Newcastle upon Tyne (see page 18).

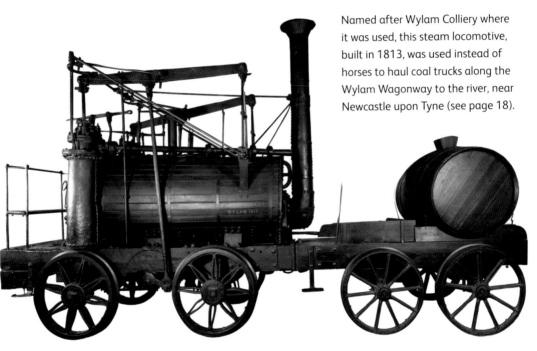

Dolly, cloned sheep, 1996–2003

Wylam Dilly, steam locomotive, designed and constructed by William Hedley, Newcastle upon Tyne, 1813

The **Connect** gallery is divided into five areas with the following themes: **Blast Off!** for space travel, **Power Up** for energy and power, **Me2** for genetics, **Robots** for robotics, and **Move It** for transport.

Black Knight rocket

A British government research rocket from the 1950s, the Black Knight was part of Britain's attempt to keep up with the arms race between the USA and the USSR.

Black Knight rocket, BK02, 1955

Communicate

Sponsored by BT

This gallery tells the story of different methods of communication. These range from simple jungle drums and smoke signals which relied on actual seeing and hearing to the electronic sophistication of the world wide web which enables instant contact across the globe.

It demonstrates how quickly technology in the field of communications moves and the difference in scale that occurs when mechanics are replaced by electronics.

Telephones in this gallery range from the very earliest, including designs by Thomas Edison, through the bulky land-line handsets for home use of the 1950s and '60s, to modern digital equipment. Different methods of communication at sea are also demonstrated through flags, morse code and satellite navigation.

All of this serves as a reminder of how fundamental rapid communication is to modern society.

K6 telephone kiosk, introduced 1936
Based on the iconic design by Giles Gilbert Scott, red telephone boxes were produced in their thousands from 1924 until the 1980s.

Shaping our World

This gallery explores four themes: increased understanding of the universe, revolutionary advances in civil engineering, the explosion in communications technology, and life-saving breakthroughs in medicine.

The displays include one of the earliest items to enter the collection, the tiny Nicol prism. Vital to 19th-century experimental science, it was used to refract light via the prism so that properties invisible to the naked eye were revealed. It was invented by the Scottish natural philosopher, William Nicol, in 1828, and this example was acquired by the Museum in 1856.

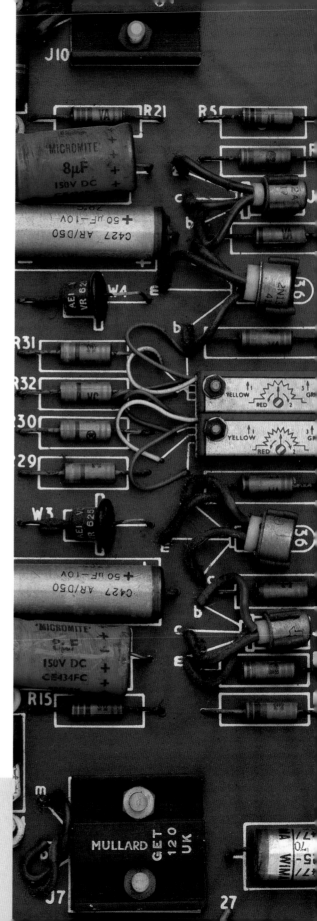

Nicol prism, England, early 19th century

Computer circuit board, LEO III, Britain, 1963–1964

Dunlop's tyre

John Boyd Dunlop's first pneumatic tyre, home-made from Arbroath sailcloth and India rubber, was made for his son's bicycle in 1888. Dunlop marketed the design successfully in the 1890s.

Baird-system television kit

John Logie Baird (1888–1946) was the first to broadcast successfully a moving monochrome image. This 'kit' was a simplified version of the Baird televisor and was on offer from the *Daily Express* newspaper in 1934.

Sir James Black

A case glitters with the medals and awards made to the Nobel prize-winning Scottish scientist, Sir James Black, for his development of beta-blockers, vital to the treatment of heart disease and other illnesses.

Baird-system television kit, Mervyn Sound and Vision Company, England, 1934

Johnny Dunlop on his bicycle with home-made pneumatic tyres, 1888

Sir James Black (1924–2010) with Nobel medal awarded in 1988

The Story of Scotland

The story of Scotland is told in the modern wing of the National Museum of Scotland. Opened in 1998, it was designed by architects Benson + Forsyth. Although contemporary in concept, the building deliberately echoes the notion of a medieval castle with its spiral staircases and towers.

The architecture is integrated with the narrative of the displays. It is split into six different levels, with a central high triangular atrium flooded with daylight. Stairs and walkways connect the galleries on the different floors and there are many unexpected perspectives throughout.

The origins of the Scottish collections lie in the Society of Antiquaries of Scotland, founded in 1780 very much in the spirit of the Enlightenment. Its collections passed into public ownership in 1858 as the original collections of the National Museum of Antiquities of Scotland. From 1891 until 1995 they were exhibited in bespoke galleries in Queen Street, Edinburgh, originally financed by the businessman and philanthropist John Ritchie Findlay. In 1985 the National Museum of Antiquities was amalgamated with the Royal Scottish Museum, bringing together the collections that can be seen today in the National Museum of Scotland.

The displays take a chronological approach, beginning with pre-history on Level 0 and finishing on the top floor, Level 6, with modern Scotland. The twists and turns of the building, however, may tempt you to detour from this timeline.

Corryvrechan Tapestry, designed by Kate Whiteford, 7.9 x 3.8 metres, hand woven by the Edinburgh Tapestry Company, 1997

The Lewis chessmen, mostly carved from walrus ivory, *c.*late 12th to early 13th century, found on the Isle of Lewis, 1831

Beginnings

The story begins billions of years ago, long before the geography of Scotland took on its present form. Here you can explore the first 3 billion years of history, and discover the origin and evolution of Scotland's landscape, flora and fauna.

The shape of the continents evolved as they moved over the surface of the earth millions of years ago. The display tracks this movement until it settled into the configuration we know today.

The impact of climate change and glaciation as life on land developed are also explained. Evidence from rocks and fossils evoke the different eras. These include the oldest known Scottish examples, the Lewisian gneiss rocks formed about 3 billion years ago, and fossils such as *Westlothiana lizzae* found in West Lothian in 1984, possibly the earliest known reptile.

There are also fossils found by pioneering Scottish geologist and writer, Hugh Miller (below) who, through his studies, made important discoveries about the age of the earth.

Panorama of tundra in Scotland, 11,750 years ago

Hugh Miller (1802–1856)

Early People

This gallery explores how people lived from around 8000 BC to AD 1100, how they used the land's resources, interacted with each other and made sense of the world. The objects for this period are of prime importance, as for most of this time there is no written record. There is virtually no trace of the people as individuals.

Four groups of figures (left) sculpted by Eduardo Paolozzi (1924–2005) stand in the introductory area, their abstraction symbolizing this gap in our understanding.

However, the displays are rich in artefacts, ranging from spectacular hoards of treasure to everyday objects used for eating, hunting, fighting and travelling. The sculpted figures signpost the four main themes: **A Generous Land** looks at the land's resources and how people used them; **Wider Horizons** explores contact with a wider world and the movement of people, goods and ideas; **Them and us** covers issues of conflict and imperialism, power and status; and **In touch with the Gods** concentrates on death, belief and ritual.

Gold torcs, Iron Age, c.300–100 BC
These torcs or neck ornaments were found near Stirling in 2009.
Supported by The Art Fund, Wolfson Foundation, Scottish Government and National Museums Scotland Charitable Trust

The greatest treasures from the Museum's archaeology collections are featured here. There are enigmatic Neolithic carved stone balls (left) dating from about 2900 BC, rich jewellery such as a 4000-year-old gold collar and the 2000-year-old gold torcs (see previous page), and a superb collection of sculpted stone slabs.

Hunterston brooch

One of the most stunning treasures is a brooch, dating from about AD 700, found at Hunterston, Ayrshire, in the early 19th century.

A highly-accomplished piece of silver casting and gilding, it reflects a mixture of Irish, Scottish and Anglo-Saxon traditions and is one of the finest survivors of its kind.

Some 200 years after it was made, its owner added an inscription on the reverse in Viking runes, which says, 'Melbrigda owns this brooch'.

Carved stone ball, Towie, Aberdeenshire, 2500 BC

Hunterston brooch, silver, gold, amber (insets incomplete), c. AD 700, found at Hunterston, Ayrshire, c.1830

The Roman occupation of Britain left its traces in Scotland. There are everyday objects from military life, as well as grander items such as the parade helmets worn by cavalrymen, the dazzling hoard of silver treasure found on Traprain Law near Edinburgh, and the dramatic sculpture of a lioness (above) devouring her human prey, probably intended to adorn a monument for a high-ranking army officer.

The arrival and spread of Christianity is reflected in the decoration of objects such as the bowls and brooches of the St Ninian's Isle treasures (right) and the bird men figures on the Papil Stone from Shetland which show how native beliefs became melded with Christianity.

Evidence of the Viking era and its impact include trading goods, weapons and finds from graves.

Lioness devouring man, Roman stone sculpture, AD 140–210, found at Cramond, near Edinburgh, in 1997

St Ninian's Isle Treasure, an 8th-century silver hoard, probably belonging to a local aristocrat, found buried in a church on St Ninian's Isle, Shetland, in 1958

Kingdom of the Scots

The **Kingdom of the Scots** gallery follows Scotland from its gradual emergence as a nation around 1100 to 1707, when the Union of the Scottish and English Parliaments created the United Kingdom of Great Britain.

The gallery explores the Gaelic heritage, the impact of Christianity and the emergence of a settled monarchy. It describes the Renaissance and the searing impact of the Reformation on the subsequent course of Scottish history, and looks at the development of the economy and Scotland's position in the wider world. Here you will find many iconic objects of Scottish history.

Cadboll cup

This cup is a superb example of the influence of the Renaissance on Scotland in the 16th century. Its design and execution are highly sophisticated and fuse Renaissance patterns with earlier Scottish style.

Monymusk reliquary

The tiny Monymusk reliquary, a portable house-shaped shrine, may date from as early as AD 750. It has powerful associations: it was once thought to have held the relics of St Columba, and to have been carried at the Battle of Bannockburn in 1314. Whatever the precise truth, it is a significant witness to early Christianity in Scotland.

Monymusk reliquary, *c.* AD 750

Cadboll cup, silver, parcel-gilt, mid-16th century
Supported by The Art Fund

Bute mazer

This mazer is strongly connected with King Robert the Bruce and his assertion of Scotland as an independent nation. Bruce led the Scots to victory against the English at Bannockburn in 1314.

As a communal drinking cup, the mazer would have been passed from guest to guest during ceremonial feasting. Its central boss shows a lion thought to represent King Robert (reigned 1306–1329), surrounded by six enamelled plaques bearing the arms of some of his supporters. The cup was modified during the 16th century, but is the earliest of Scotland's surviving mazers.

Lewis chessmen

The Lewis chessmen are one of Scotland's most significant archaeological finds, discovered on the Isle of Lewis in 1831. There are 93 pieces, made mostly of intricately carved walrus ivory. These are now in the collections of the National Museum of Scotland and British Museum.

Their history excites much speculation, but it is believed they are Scandinavian in origin, and that they perhaps belonged to a merchant travelling from Norway to Ireland, or to a local aristocrat.

Thought to have been made in Trondheim, Norway, during the late 12th and early 13th century, they may have been buried in Lewis for safekeeping en route to being traded in Ireland. At that time, Lewis owed allegiance to the Kingdom of Norway, not Scotland.

Bute mazer, communal drinking cup, Scottish, 14th century, with silver rim, 16th century
On loan from The Bute Collection at Mount Stuart

Lewis chessmen, mostly carved from walrus ivory, c.late 12th to early 13th century, found on the Isle of Lewis, 1831

Mary, Queen of Scots

The life and times of Scotland's most famous female monarch, Mary, Queen of Scots (reigned 1542–1567), are represented through items associated with her, including jewellery, coins, medals and books.

The 'Queen Mary' harp, a West Highland clarsach, was thought to have been gifted by the Queen to a supporter. Made in the 15th century, this small harp is a very rare survivor of the definitive instrument for the Gaelic culture and music of the period. You can see two of the surviving three harps of this type in the display.

Mary's father and mother, King James V and the French princess, Mary of Guise, epitomized the influence of the Renaissance on Scotland, culminating in James's creation of a Renaissance-style court at Stirling Castle. Carvings, furniture and silver demonstrate the increasingly sophisticated techniques and changing motifs of craftsmen and artists of the period.

Enamelled locket with cameo of Mary, Queen of Scots, late 16th century

Clarsach harp, known as the 'Queen Mary' harp, with characteristic West Highland decoration, c.1450

Mary, Queen of Scots (1542–1587)

The religious strand in Scottish history is shown in the representation of the saints of the Catholic church in statues, carvings and on decoration, including Andrew (right), the patron saint of Scotland.

Saint Andrew

From about the 13th century Saint Andrew and his cross, the saltire, have been symbols of the Scottish nation. This oak-carved figure was possibly once part of a screen or altarpiece.

The Covenanters

The disruption of the Protestant movement and the subsequent religious upheavals are explored, with particularly interesting material dating from the Covenanting Wars of the 17th century.

The Covenanters were staunch supporters of the democracy of the Presbyterian Church. They preferred to be outlawed and to fight their cause, rather than to suffer the imposition of the hierarchy of the English Episcopalian church.

The displays include the banners of the movement and the terrifying mask worn as disguise by one of their most charismatic leaders, Alexander Peden.

Crozier of St Fillan
A 15th-century silver-gilt casing houses the remains of a crozier, or staff, associated with an 8th-century Christian saint, Fillan.

St Andrew, oak carving, Low Countries, c.1500

Mask and wig of Covenanting minister, Alexander Peden (1626–1686)

In the 17th century, Scotland expanded economically and culturally. Trading abroad reached new heights and, with it, the ambition to found a Scottish colony. The Darien Scheme, funded by Scots, made a disastrous choice of location for its expeditions of 1698 and 1699, landing in the swampy regions of Central America. The resultant financial collapse was a critical factor in the negotiations which led to the Union of the Parliaments of Scotland and England in 1707, a union which lasted until 1999.

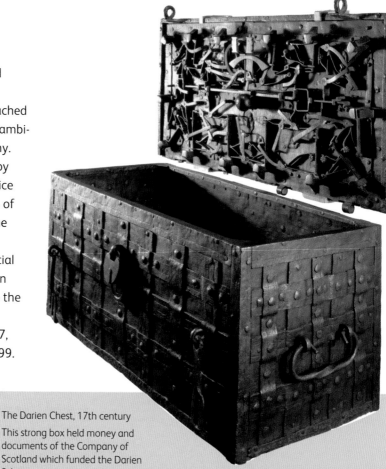

Book plate showing a graphic scheme of the Scottish Parliament in session, c.1680–1685, from Chatelaine's *Atlas Historique*, 1720

The Darien Chest, 17th century

This strong box held money and documents of the Company of Scotland which funded the Darien Scheme.

Scotland Transformed

The displays illustrate some of the contrasts in a society which became renowned for the calibre of its intellectual advancement. This was the Age of Enlightenment, a period of great change, during which Scotland was transformed from a predominantly rural, medieval society into the beginnings of an urban, modern one. This happened in the course of the 18th and early 19th centuries.

Bonnie Prince Charlie

The last battle fought on British soil was the Battle of Culloden on 16 April 1746. Prince Charles Edward Stuart, better known to history as Bonnie Prince Charlie, tried and failed catastrophically to assert his Stuart dynasty's claim to the throne of England, Scotland and Ireland against the Hanoverian King George II.

There are many items associated with the Jacobite cause and its mythology. A highlight is Prince Charles Edward's beautifully-crafted silver travelling canteen (above), lost at the Battle of Culloden. This fine piece of work by an Edinburgh silversmith may have been a 21st birthday present.

Bonnie Prince Charlie's travelling canteen, made by Ebenezer Oliphant, Edinburgh, 1740–1741

Prince Charles Edward Stuart (1720–1788), by Antonio David, 1732 [detail]
Scottish National Portrait Gallery

The slower pace of change in rural life is shown in the cruck-framed house and other primitive domestic and everyday items, the patterns and materials of which had not changed much in generations. The cruck-frame technique, in which the structure of the building depended on two or more timber 'A frames' going from the top of the building down to the ground, had lasted from medieval times.

The 18th century saw the rapid advance of new industries and trades. Coal and iron supported the development of manufacture, while the huge tobacco and sugar trade led to the expansion of Glasgow as a port and city.

Newcomen engine

In the centre of the gallery is the enormous steam engine of a type originally designed by Thomas Newcomen in 1712. This important invention enabled water to be pumped out from coal mines, thus solving the problem of flooding. It is one of a number of examples in the gallery of machines that supported Scotland's industrial expansion. The Newcomen is one of the very few of its kind still in working order.

Newcomen engine at Caprington Colliery, Ayrshire. It was used to pump water from 1811 until 1910.

The same Newcomen engine in the Museum (right).

In the early 19th century, tartan, which had been banned after the Jacobite rebellion, enjoyed new popularity. The visit of George IV to Edinburgh in 1822 signalled a resurgence of a particular version of Scottishness, and the king himself sported some splendid tartan outfits.

The manufacture of tartan grew to meet fashionable demand alongside the production of other textiles, such as cotton, jute and tweed.

The displays illustrate the growing emphasis upon and sophistication of material comfort.

The strength of the continued influence of religion is also shown, with objects illustrating the vigorous religious debate which split the Scottish church into many different factions and continued well into the 19th century, culminating in the Disruption of the established Church of Scotland in 1843.

Uniform of the Royal Company of Archers, early 18th century
Wearing tartan was associated with pro-Jacobite sentiments during this period.

A group of silver urns by Scottish silversmiths, 18th century. This ovoid design was unique to Scotland.

Industry and Empire

In the 19th century, the British Empire loomed large in the Scottish consciousness. It drove the expansion of its industry until the country became one of the most industrialized in the world, manufacturing and exporting goods all over the globe.

Scots looked abroad for opportunity and many left the country, some to escape from poverty, but others to find a wider application of their skills and education. By the 1890s Glasgow had become the second city of Empire.

The displays in this gallery examine three critical industries: railway engineering, whisky production and shipbuilding.

The great bulk of the Leith-built *Ellesmere* steam locomotive gleams darkly, while close by you will see the bright copper contours of a traditional whisky still. The models of ships that demostrate the strength of the ship-building industry are complemented by displays that highlight achievements in Scottish engineering, such as lighthouse construction, road building, printing and paper-making.

SS *Nerbudda*, model, cargo ship, built on the Clyde, 1883

Rotary printing press, Edinburgh, 1850
The first of its kind, this press was made in Edinburgh by the printer Thomas Nelson. It was exhibited at the Great Exhibition in London in 1851.

Ellesmere locomotive

The *Ellesmere* was built in 1861 by Hawthorns and Co. of Leith for a colliery at Leigh in Lancashire. When the colliery finally closed in 1957, *Ellesmere* was the oldest working steam locomotive in Britain.

Robert Stevenson

For five generations the Stevenson name was the most famous in the construction and development of lighthouses and harbours. The outstanding achievement of Robert Stevenson was the Bell Rock lighthouse, built in tidal waters off Angus on the east coast of Scotland, between 1807 and 1810.

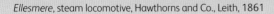

Ellesmere, steam locomotive, Hawthorns and Co., Leith, 1861

Bell Rock lighthouse,
designed by Robert Stevenson, model, 1822

Robert Stevenson (1772–1850)

Industry gave rise to rapid urban development and great changes to people's lives. Deprivation and overcrowding were common, but a new consumer society was beginning to emerge.

When the famous Victorian artist, Edwin Landseer, painted his great work *Monarch of the Glen* in 1851, it epitomized a romantic concept of Scotland as a rural country, a view distinctly at odds with the reality.

Monarch of the Glen, Edwin Landseer (1802–1873), oil on canvas, London, 1881
Lent by Diageo

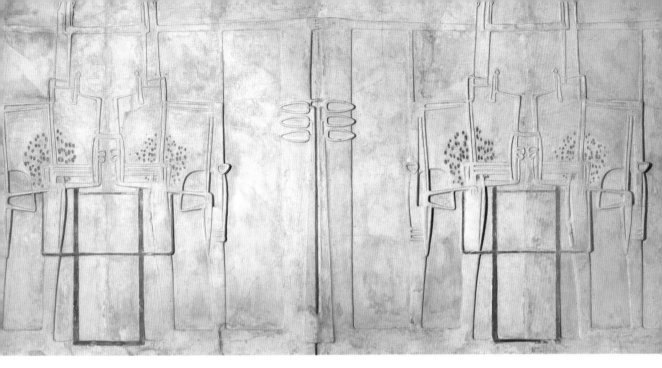

Scottish artists such as Charles Rennie Mackintosh (1868–1928), Phoebe Anna Traquair (1852–1936) and Robert Lorimer (1864–1929) became leading members of contemporary artistic movements, and the displays include examples of their work alongside the work of their contemporaries.

You can see Mackintosh's Art Nouveau furniture and wall panels (above) for the Willow Tea Rooms in Glasgow, Marion Henderson Wilson's Arts and Crafts-style mantle clock, and Lorimer's designs for the National War Memorial at Edinburgh Castle.

Mantle clock, Marion Henderson Wilson (1869–1956), Glasgow, c.1900

Willowwood, plasterwork panels from a decorative frieze, designed by Charles Rennie Mackintosh, Glasgow, 1903

Scotland and the World

Scots have a long tradition of adventure and exploration. These displays look at the Scottish impact in India, America, Australasia and Africa.

Famous names from the history of exploration include Dr John Rae in the Arctic, and Captain James Cook in the Pacific. You can see snowshoes which belonged to Rae and a ceremonial feather collar from Tahiti that was presented to Cook.

The display shows emigration from Scotland in its many forms: the dispossessed seeking new land, the skilled in search of opportunities, the trader creating business, and the missionary looking for souls. The Highland Clearances, in which tenants were forcibly evicted by their landlords, caused successive waves of emigration during the 18th and 19th centuries.

Innovators

Scots have made their mark in many different ways in the arts and sciences.

Representing Scottish literary tradition, there is a glass scratched with words by the poet Robert Burns (1759–1796), and an hour-glass used by Sir Walter Scott (1771–1832) to time his writing.

Objects representing science and engineering include instruments owned by General Sir Thomas Makdougall Brisbane (1773–1860), Governor of New South Wales and astronomer, and examples of early television designed by John Logie Baird (1888–1946).

Snowshoes, made and used in 1851 by John Rae during his Arctic exploration
University of Edinburgh Collections

John Rae (1813–1893)
Scottish National Portrait Gallery

Coronach in the backwoods,
by George W. Simson, 1859
A sentimental portrayal of an emigrant family in Canada.

LINE UP, BOYS!

ENLIST TO-DAY.

Scotland: A Changing Nation

This exhibition explores the changes of the 20th century and their impact on Scotland. Major themes include the effects of war, the development of the economy, social change and emigration, and political evolution.

It provides insight into some of the challenges of poverty, social deprivation and industrial collapse that have triggered and influenced the pace of change. It also emphasizes the underlying continuity with the past and how this shapes the future.

One Nation, Five Million Voices

Through personal stories, film, music, poetry and objects, you will discover both the familiar and less expected aspects of Scottish life. The film *One Nation, Five Million Voices* presents Scots and other nationalities talking about what it means to be Scottish, and how they perceive the country.

Recruitment poster, 1914

Victoria Cross, awarded to Piper Daniel Laidlaw, 25 September 1915
This highest military honour was awarded for gallantry at the Battle of Loos during the First World War. Under enemy fire, Laidlaw played his pipes and encouraged his company 'over the top' into battle.

Scottish celebrities, such as the singer Lulu, actor Ewan McGregor and writer Ian Rankin, have contributed material – a stage dress, the screenplay of *Trainspotting*, and a manuscript respectively – adding to an exciting display of contemporary culture.

A new tartan design, created with the help of a luggage X-ray machine by an emigrant Australian artist, Jill Kinnear, signifies the modern Scottish diaspora, the millions of people all over the world who are proud to claim some kind of connection to Scotland.

The political story runs from the early days of the Labour movement, led by Keir Hardy, to the opening of the Scottish Parliament in July 1999 and the occupation of its new building at Holyrood in October 2004.

Finally, the achievements of contemporary Scots in many different fields are celebrated, including science, culture and sport, a reminder of the vibrant life of the nation and its international reach.

Hillman Imp Deluxe motor car, built by Rootes, Linwood, Scotland
Operational from 1963 to 1981, the factory at Linwood was an attempt to build new industry in Scotland.

Dounreay Nuclear Reactor, by Kate Williams and John Floyd, kiln cast using uranium glass lit with ultra-violet light, 2006
The reactor at Dounreay was in operation from 1959 to 1977 as an experimental alternative source of power.

National Museum of Scotland: the wing housing
the **Story of Scotland**, completed in 1998.

A Short History

Two strands of history come together in the development of National Museums Scotland* – the desire to have a museum that reflects Scottish history and one that demonstrates international culture, natural and physical science, and decorative art for Scotland.

The Society of Antiquaries of Scotland was founded in 1780, in the spirit of the Enlightenment, to collect mainly the archaeology of Scotland. Its collections passed into public ownership in 1858 as the original collections of the National Museum of Antiquities of Scotland. These were housed from 1891 until 1995 in specially-built galleries in Finlay Buildings, Queen Street, Edinburgh.

In 1985 the National Museum of Antiquities was amalgamated with the Royal Scottish Museum. The latter was founded in 1854 as the Industrial Museum of Scotland and reflected the impetus of Victorian ideals of education. It began international collecting and research, as well as forming close links to the collections and teaching of the University of Edinburgh. Renamed the Edinburgh Museum of Science and Art, it opened in its first bespoke buildings, designed by Francis Fowke, in Chambers Street in 1866, where it remains today. From 1904 until 1997 it was known as the Royal Scottish Museum.

The 1985 amalgamation created the National Museums of Scotland (rebranded National Museums Scotland in 2006), the largest multi-disciplinary museum in Scotland, with collections of international importance.

A major extension using contemporary architectural idiom was added to create the Museum of Scotland which opened in 1998. This tells the story of Scotland from earliest times to the present day.

Between 2004 and 2011 the Royal Museum ('Scottish' was dropped in 1997 to avoid confusion with the new Museum) underwent a transformative project to revitalize its Victorian galleries for the 21st century. After three years of partial closure it reopened to enormous acclaim on 29 July 2011. The project has finally and successfully united the two strands of the Museum's history in a single entity – the National Museum of Scotland. Housed in its glorious building and with displays that celebrate its collections for modern audiences, the Museum can fulfil its mission of 'Inspiring people; connecting Scotland to the world and the world to Scotland'.

View of the Main Hall of the Edinburgh Museum of Science and Art – now the Grand Gallery of the National Museum of Scotland, c.1867.

* National Museums Scotland is our corporate name covering all our sites. The National Museum of Scotland in Chambers Street, Edinburgh, is our main site.

Imagine (Level 1)

Designed for families with young children, this gallery offers a chance to make music, tell stories and create art inspired by real objects from around the world. Invent your own shadow puppet tale, or get cosy in our story corner with books, story bags and puppets. Dress up in outfits from different cultures, or find some friends to help you make a Chinese dragon dance.

Adventure Planet (Level 5)

What will you unearth in our interactive nature gallery? Take part in a 'dino-dig' or dress up to explore the extreme environment in the Arctic, under the sea, or in the jungle. Measure yourself against a stegosaurus or identify mystery animals from their smells and other clues, and find out what camouflage you need to hide from predators.

National Museums Scotland

www.nms.ac.uk/scotland

National Museum of Scotland

Chambers Street
Edinburgh EH1 1JF

Open daily: **10.00–17.00**
Admission **free**, donations welcome
For information and bookings, call:
0300 123 6789

Keep up to date: sign up for our e-bulletins at:
www.nms.ac.uk/signup

Support us

National Museums Scotland is a registered charity. If you enjoyed your visit, please make a donation or join as a Museum Member. The money we raise helps to increase access to our collections.

Become a National Museums Member and enjoy exclusive benefits:

- Free entry and priority access to charging exhibitions
- Free or discounted entry to all our charging museums
- Exclusive Member events
- Discounts in all our cafés and shops
- Be the first to know what's on with regular mailings

National Museums Scotland

National Museum of Scotland, Edinburgh
National War Museum, Edinburgh Castle
National Museum of Flight, East Lothian
National Museum of Rural Life, East Kilbride
National Museum of Costume, Dumfries

Visitor information

Learning Centre

The three-storey Learning Centre is the hub of inspiring activities for all ages, 7 days a week. To find out what's on, check our information screens, pick up a brochure, or ask staff for details.

Eating and drinking

Our **Balcony Café** and **Museum Brasserie** are open daily from 10.00–17.00 for tea, coffee, home-baking, snacks and meals. Call the **Brasserie** on **0131 247 4040** to book a table. The **Tower Restaurant** is open all day for lunch, afternoon tea and dinner: reservations can be made on **0131 225 3003**.

Shopping

Visit our shops to buy something to remind you of your visit. We have an extensive selection of imaginative gifts, souvenirs, toys and books. You can also shop online at: **www.nms.ac.uk/shop**

Info Zone and Research Library

Drop in to our **Info Zone** or **Research Library** on Level 3 to learn more about the Museum and our remarkable collections.

Access

Wheelchair loan, special tours and handling sessions are available by arrangement.
Visit **www.nms.ac.uk/access** for more information.

Events and entertaining

From dinners to private exhibition views, conferences to weddings, we can deliver a great event in our stunning spaces. Call **0131 247 4113** or visit
www.nms.ac.uk/hospitality

Sulphur butterfly, *Phoebis argante*,
Central and Southern America

National Museums Scotland
Scottish Charity, No. SC011130